World of WOW (Wonder)

I didn't know that

Get ready to hear your kids say, "Wow! I didn't know that!" as they dive into this fun, informative, question-answering series of books! Students—and teachers and parents—will learn things about the world around them that they never knew before!

This approach to education seeks to promote an interest in learning by answering questions kids have always wondered about. When books answer questions that kids already want to know the answers to, kids love to read those books, fostering a love for reading and learning, the true keys to lifelong education.

Colorful graphics are labeled and explained to connect with visual learners, while in-depth explanations of each subject will connect with those who prefer reading or listening as their learning style.

This educational series makes learning fun through many levels of interaction. The entertaining information combined with fantastic illustrations promote learning and retention, while question and answer boxes reinforce the subject matter to promote higher order thinking.

Teachers and parents love this series because it engages young people, sparking an interest and desire in learning. It doesn't feel like work to learn about a new subject with books this interactive and interesting.

This set of books will be an addition to your home or classroom library that everyone will enjoy. And, before you know it, you too will be saying, "Wow! I didn't know that!"

"People cannot learn by having information pressed into their brains. Knowledge has to be sucked into the brain, not pushed in. First, one must create a state of mind that craves knowledge, interest, and wonder. You can teach only by creating an urge to know." - Victor Weisskopf

© 2014 Flowerpot Press

Contents under license from Aladdin Books Ltd.

Flowerpot Press
142 2nd Avenue North
Franklin, TN 37064

Flowerpot Press is a Division of Kamalu LLC, Franklin, TN, U.S.A. and
Flowerpot Children's Press, Inc., Oakville, ON, Canada.

ISBN 978-1-4867-0340-1

Concept, editorial, and design by
David West Children's Books.

Designer:
Robert Perry

Illustrators:
Francis Phillipps, Ian Thompson, Rob Shone, Jo Moore

American Edition Editor:
Johannah Gilman Paiva

American Redesign:
Jonas Fearon Bell

Copy Editor:
Kimberly Horg

Educational Consultant:
Jim Heacock

Printed in China.

WORLD OF
WoW
WONDER

I didn't know that

You can jump higher on the moon

CCCP

I didn't know that

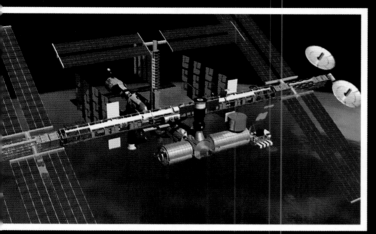

Introduction

Did you know that one day people will go to Mars? That trips to space will be possible for everybody? That aliens might really exist?

Discover for yourself amazing facts about space exploration, from the earliest attempts to today's amazing International Space Station.

Watch for this symbol, which means there is a fun project for you to try.

True or false? Watch for this symbol and try to answer the question before reading on for the answer.

Don't forget to check the borders for extra amazing facts!

I didn't know that

rockets can travel at 25,000 mph (40,234 km/h). This is the speed needed to escape Earth's gravity and enter space. A steady 18,000 mph (28,968 km/h) keeps the rocket in orbit. Modern rockets are used for launching space probes and satellites.

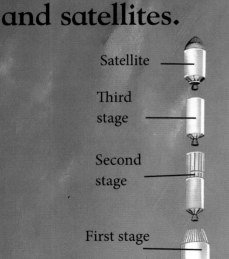

Satellite

Third stage

Second stage

First stage

Solid-fuel boosters

The rocket is pushed into space by three stages that burn up and fall away one by one.

Werner von Braun was the German inventor of the dead V-2 rocket. Later, he became the chief designer of space rockets in the United States.

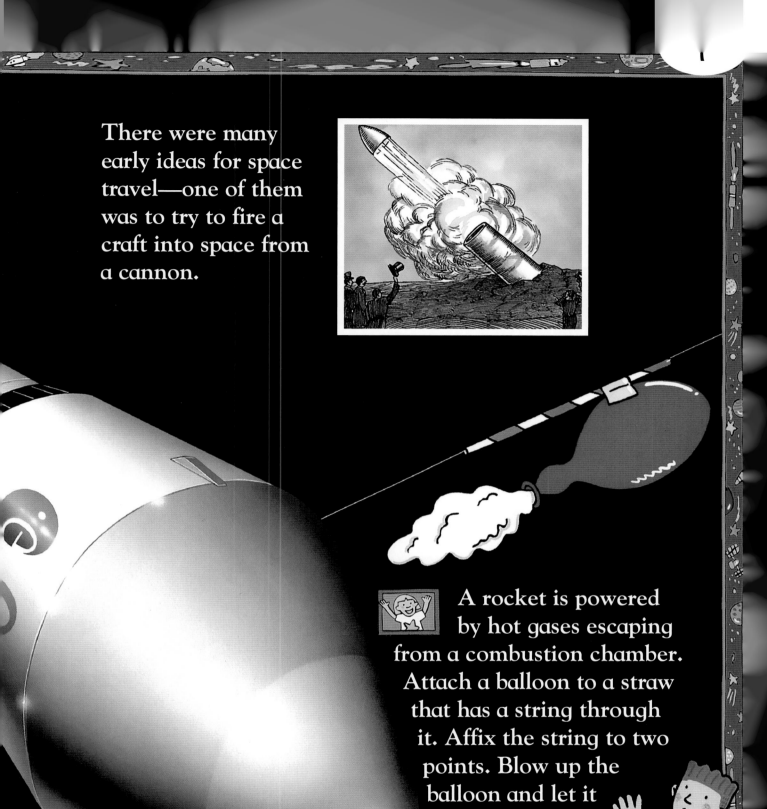

There were many early ideas for space travel—one of them was to try to fire a craft into space from a cannon.

A rocket is powered by hot gases escaping from a combustion chamber. Attach a balloon to a straw that has a string through it. Affix the string to two points. Blow up the balloon and let it go. Escaping air pushes it up like a rocket.

The Chinese invented rockets nearly 1,000 years ago.

I didn't know that

there is no air in space. As you leave the Earth behind, the air gets thinner and thinner. By the time you reach space–100 miles (161 km) up–there is no air at all. Space is a vacuum.

Can you find the a nut?

True or false?
Flying fragments could kill an unprotected astronaut—if unbearable heat, cold, or radiation didn't strike first.

Answer: True
It's dangerous out there!
In 1996, a British-built satellite was smashed by a briefcase-sized piece of the *Ariane* rocket.

Nothing burns without oxygen. Watch a candle go out when it has used all the oxygen in the jar. (Once the flame goes out, the gases cool, and the water rises.) Because space has no air, spacecraft carry liquid oxygen to burn fuel.

!
WARNING
ADULT
HELP NEEDED

Use coins to hold up jar.

The cosmonaut Alexei Leonov made the first-ever space walk way back in March 1965. He floated in space for 20 minutes before struggling back into the tiny spacecraft, *Voshkod 2.*

...one giant leap for mankind.

I didn't know that

you can jump higher on the Moon. Astronauts on the Moon can run and leap much farther than on the Earth. This is because the Moon's gravity is a lot weaker.

Your weight on the Moon is one-sixth of your Earth weight. Can you figure out how much you would weigh if you were standing on the Moon?

Jules Verne wrote a book called *From the Earth to the Moon* in 1865. He didn't realize that there was no air on the Moon!

Can you find the spaceship?

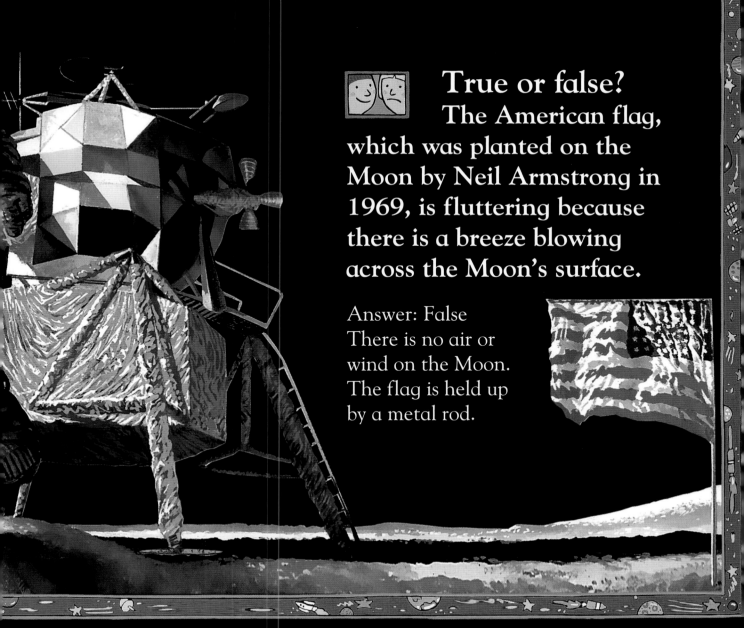

True or false?

The American flag, which was planted on the Moon by Neil Armstrong in 1969, is fluttering because there is a breeze blowing across the Moon's surface.

Answer: False
There is no air or wind on the Moon. The flag is held up by a metal rod.

The Moon has wide plains, which are called "seas" but there is no water!

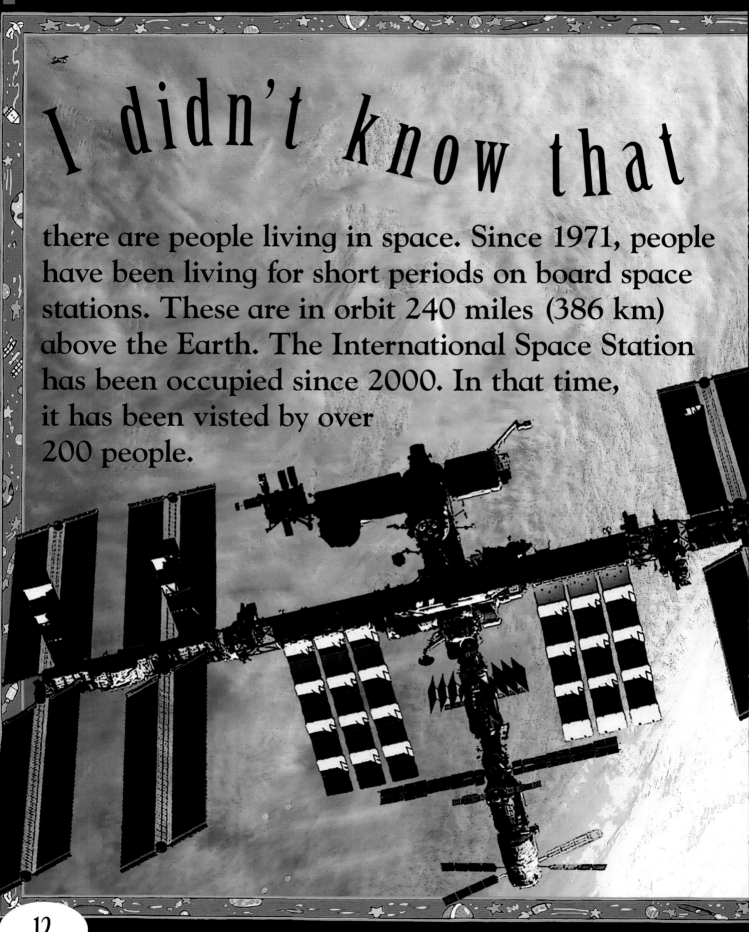

I didn't know that

there are people living in space. Since 1971, people have been living for short periods on board space stations. These are in orbit 240 miles (386 km) above the Earth. The International Space Station has been occupied since 2000. In that time, it has been visted by over 200 people.

True or false?
The International Space Station is as big as a football field and weighs close to a million pounds.

Answer: True
The Space Station, including its large solar rays, spans the area of a U.S. football field: with the end zones, and weighs 924,739 pounds (419,455 kg). It has more room than a six-bedroom house, and has two bathrooms, a gym, and a 360-degree bay window.

Can you find a *Soyuz* spacecraft?

Astronauts need strict routines for working and resting to make life in space seem more normal. They work 12 hours a day and exercise 2.5 hours a day to keep their muscles strong and be able to do their jobs well.

Spiders, fish, monkeys, and dogs have all tried floating in space.

I didn't know that

astronauts are water-cooled. Their underwear is threaded with liquid-filled tubes to keep their bodies at a steady temperature. Otherwise, they might boil or freeze outside the spacecraft.

An astronaut can spend several hours outside the spacecraft in an MMU (Manned Maneuvering Unit). The space suit and the MMU form a life-support system with oxygen and cooling fluids, a snack to eat, and even a diaper!

Can you find the second astronaut?

1. Multilayered space suit

2. Liquid-cooled undergarment

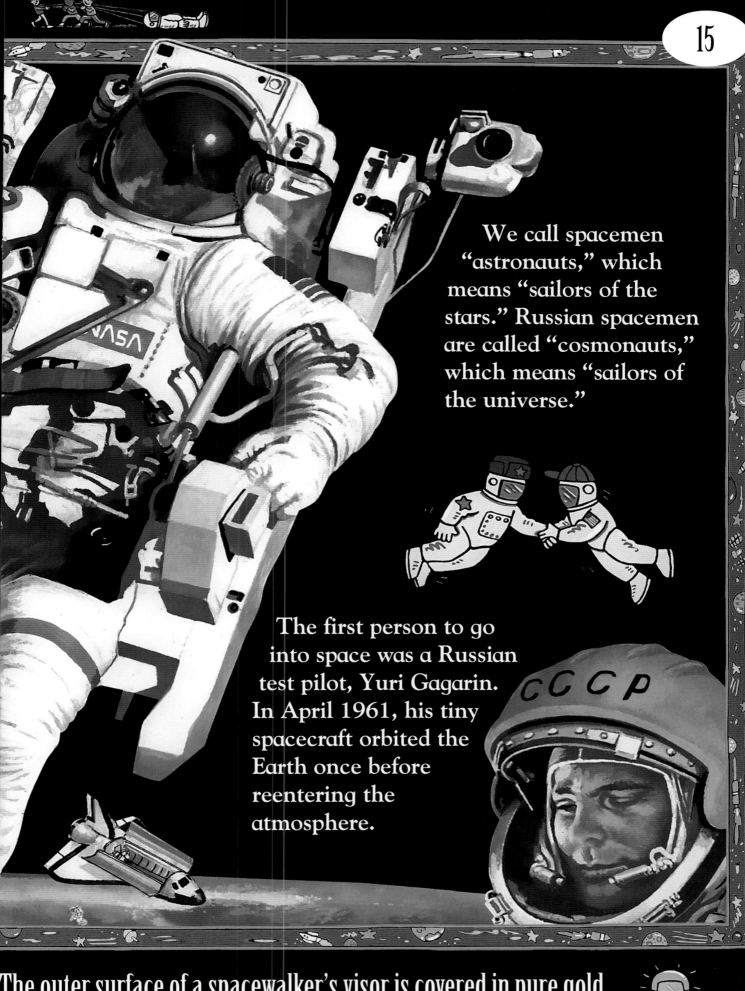

We call spacemen "astronauts," which means "sailors of the stars." Russian spacemen are called "cosmonauts," which means "sailors of the universe."

The first person to go into space was a Russian test pilot, Yuri Gagarin. In April 1961, his tiny spacecraft orbited the Earth once before reentering the atmosphere.

CCCP

The outer surface of a spacewalker's visor is covered in pure gold.

! The Space Shuttle could be flown to its launch site on a jumbo jet's back.

I didn't know that

heatproof tiles prevent a spacecraft from burning up when it reenters the Earth's atmosphere. This way, it can be used again.

Can you find the lost tile?

After reentry, landing a spacecraft safely is the hardest part of the journey. The first space travelers had to abandon their craft four miles (6.4 km) above the Earth and parachute to safety.

Three astronauts escaped from an explosion on board *Apollo 13*. But tragically, seven astronauts were killed in 1986 when the *Challenger* blew up; seven more astronauts died in 2003 when the shuttle disintegrated on reentry.

True or false?

NASA's Space Shuttle is still in use today.

Answer: False
The Space Shuttle was retired from service upon the conclusion of *Atlantis'* final flight on July 21, 2011.

There were over 135 successful Shuttle trips into space from 1981 to 2011.

I didn't know that

there's a telescope in space. A space telescope can view space without Earth's atmosphere getting in the way. The Hubble Space Telescope was put into orbit 384 miles (618 km) above the Earth in 1990.

The Italian Galileo Galilei (1564-1642) was one of the earliest scientists to build a telescope. He first discovered that there were four moons orbiting Jupiter.

True or false?
The Hubble Space Telescope (HST) can "see" a coin 400 miles (644 km) away.

Answer: True
It can also see galaxies in space that are 14 billion light-years away—as they were 14 billion years ago!

Can you find the planet Mars?

The HST is a tube 562 inches (1,427 cm) long and 196 inches (498 cm) across. Mirrors reflect the light from distant galaxies onto electronic instruments that send signals back to Earth. The signals are then converted into pictures of the galaxies.

I didn't know that

satellites are powered by the Sun. As they travel around the Earth, satellites need electricity to power them. This is supplied by solar cells. Large arrays of solar panels convert the energy from the Sun into electricity to replenish the satellites' batteries.

Can you find the Space Shuttle?

True or false?
Satellites eventually fall back to Earth.

Answer: False
Only those satellites in low orbits fall back to Earth and burn up. Those farther out in space will remain in orbit for millions of years.

Sputnik 2 had a dog named Laika on its cr

Satellites orbit the Earth. Earth's gravity stops them from flying off into space. Attach a ball to a piece of string and spin it around. The pull of the string is like the pull of gravity. The ball's speed keeps it in orbit. Pull the string in as you spin and see what happens. Just as you have to move faster to keep the ball in motion, planets closer to the Sun have to move faster —to avoid being pulled by the Sun's gravity.

The first-ever artificial satellite was called *Sputnik 1*. There were 10 *Sputniks* in all. They were built by the former Soviet Union, and the first one was launched in 1957.

I didn't know that

astronauts fix broken satellites
in space. Space engineers are
specially trained to recover
faulty satellites and repair them.
Members of the repair team have
to be able to work in zero gravity
while wearing space suits.

Can
you find
another satellite?

Some of the
astronauts' training
takes place in a
water tank so they
can get used to
floating about.

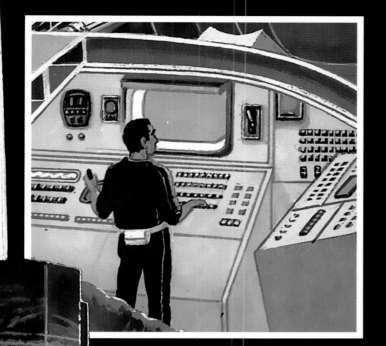

True or false?
Spacecrafts have arms and hands.

Answer: True
The jointed robot arm on a
spacecraft has a hand
on the end that can
grip objects in space. It is
operated from inside the craft.

An astronaut with
an MMU becomes a
human satellite. The word
"satellite" describes one thing
that is in orbit around another.
For example, the Moon is a
satellite of the Earth.

I didn't know that

a *Viking* has landed on Mars. Two *Viking* probes went to Mars in 1976. The landers were like mini-laboratories that took photos and analyzed samples. They sent information to Earth for six years. Mars is currently host to five functioning spacecraft: three in orbit and two on its surface.

True or false?
There are signs of life on Mars.

Answer: True
Tiny volcanic organisms have been found in a meteorite that came from Mars. Recent evidence indicates that water once flowed in streams on Mars. In 2013, NASA's *Curiosity* rover discovered that Mars' soil contains between 1.5 and 3% water by mass.

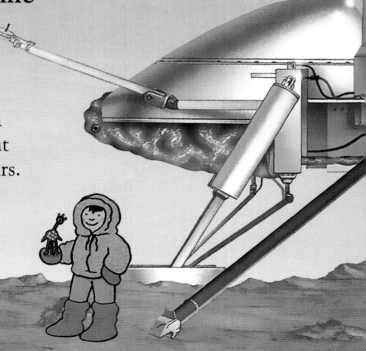

Did you know that in 2012 a Mars laboratory arrived at Mars? Its job is to collect soil and rock samples of the red, rocky surface to help us understand more about this amazing planet.

Can you find a *Viking* mother ship?

Mars really is red, from the iron oxide (rust) in the soil.

I didn't know that

a robot is lost in space. The *Voyager* space probes launched in 1977 visited Jupiter, Saturn, Uranus, and Neptune. Although lost far out in the Solar System, they act like robots and still send signals to Earth.

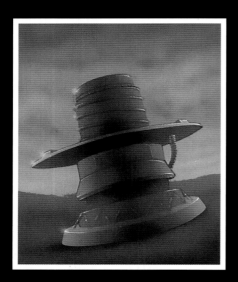

True or false?
Probes have only landed on Mars.

Answer: False
Probes have landed on Venus and relayed information to Earth before being crushed by the Venusian atmosphere.

Pictures of Halley's Comet, sent back by the space probe *Giotto,* showed that the nucleus (or center) is a city-sized lump of ice and dust.

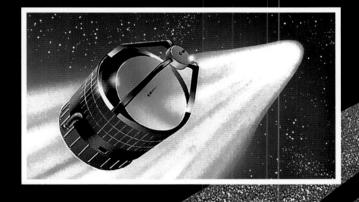

The *Pioneer* space probes carry a "calling card" for aliens. It has maps showing the position of Earth and pictures of humans.

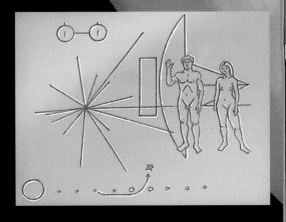

! The *Voyager* spacecraft operate on nuclear power.

I didn't know that

one day people will land on Mars. People could live on Mars in the future, but they would have to stay under cover. Its arid, rocky, cold environment would not be easy to live in—imagine volcanoes bigger than the ones in Hawaii, but temperatures colder than Alaska.

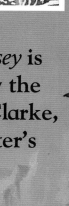

The famous film *2001: A Space Odyssey* is based on a story by the writer Arthur C. Clarke, and mentions Jupiter's moon, Europa.

The International Space Station is not just an orbiting laboratory—it provides a home to those exploring space. Over 200 explorers have visited since 2000!

Space travel has come a long way. Less than a hundred years ago, intelligent people thought a journey to the Moon was a crazy idea!

The journey alone to Mars would take nearly two years.

Glossary

Astronomer
Someone who studies the stars and the planets.

Atmosphere (Earth's)
The protective layer of gases around the planet.

Combustion chamber
The part of a rocket where the fuel and oxidizer combine and burn.

Galaxy
A collection of millions of stars.

Gravity
The natural "pull" of one object on another. Earth's gravity keeps us on the ground.

Light-year
5,880,000 miles (9,461,000 km the distance traveled by a ray of light in one year.

Meteorite
A piece of rock or metal from space that lands on Earth.

Nuclear power
Space probes on long journeys carry nuclear power packs that convert the energy of radioactive plutonium into electrical power.

Orbit
The path around a star or a planet taken by an object moving through space.

Organism
Any life-form, including those with very few cells, such as bacteria and viruses.

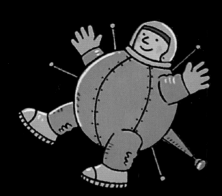

Solar System
Our Sun and everything that
orbits around it.

Space probe
A fully-automated spacecraft
that sends back information.

Radiation
Harmful radiation contains
particles and gamma rays
emitted after a nuclear
reaction.

Satellite
Artificial satellites orbiting
in space are used for
communications, navigation,
weather reports, and spying.

Index

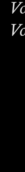